William Minturn

Aaron Burr

A Drama in four Acts

William Minturn

Aaron Burr
A Drama in four Acts

ISBN/EAN: 9783337336875

Printed in Europe, USA, Canada, Australia, Japan

Cover: Foto ©Thomas Meinert / pixelio.de

More available books at **www.hansebooks.com**

A

DRAMA,

IN FOUR ACTS.

BY

(DEFENTHY WRIGHT) WILLIAM MINTURN.

NEW YORK:

METROPOLITAN JOB PRINT, No. 28 ANN STREET.

1878.

CHARACTERS.

AARON BURR.................................

GENERAL WILKINSON........................

HARMAN BLENNERHASSETT.................

DOCTOR BOLLMAN..........................

BARON BASTROP............................

NEMO.......................................

ZEKIEL GREEN.........·...................

SAMBO......................................

PADDY......................................

CHAPLAIN...................................

GAMBLER ....

SOLDIER....................................

MESSENGER.................................

ALICE LEIGHTON........... ....

MARGARET..................................

MRS. BLENNERHASSETT.....................

PATIENCE GREEN...........................

SOLDIERS AND GUESTS.

AARON BURR.

ACT I.

SCENE I.

Burr's Library at Richmond Hill. Fire Place with fire, etc.
Elegant and substantial furniture. A life-size painting of
Hamilton. Pair of pistols on mantel,

(*Sambo discovered arranging room, etc., L*)

SAMBO. Dar's somethin' gwine wrong in dis yeah house, shua
—Mas' Aaron aint de same man dat he was—Ebber since he done
dat shootin' dat ebbery pusson's talkin' 'bout, he hab a face as long
as a funeral percession, an' he talk to hisself 'till dis niggah tink
he gwine stark, bodily naked fool, shua. Dar yest'day mornin' I's
done ketch him stannin' jest here, dis way, wid one ob dem shootin' machines in one hand, an' den he say somethin' under his bref
like, an' den he shoot away at dat ar picture ob Mas' Hamilton
tell he make a half dozen holes clean through and through. I's a
plain, straight-sided ole niggah, I is, an' I wont stan' no sich
foolin' like dat. I jist hab to git Mas' Aaron a talkin' to 'bout it.
Den he hab a lot ob strange gemmen come heah an' talk an' talk
an' talk all night instead ob gwine to bed. I's a cute niggah, I is,
an' I jist know somethin' gwine to happen. Things aint right—
min' what I say (*at window L.*), sartin' shua, when dis niggah
mak' his min' up—why, who's dat jis clumb ober de garden wall?
I speck I better jist go out dar an' take a look 'round—folks don't

come into a gemmen's garden dat way 'less dey means bissness.
I's a cute niggah, I is, sartin, shua.

(Going R.)

BURR. *(Without L.)* Sambo! Sambo!

SAMBO. *(Stopping.)* Dat's Mas' Aaron.

BURR. *(Without.)* Sambo, you black rascal!

SAMBO. Here I is. I's comin', sah.

(Enter Burr in riding trim, with military hat. Cloak on arm. L. upper.)

BURR. Coming! Why were you not out by the gate to take my horse? Here, take these. *(Tosses cloak and hat to Sambo.)* Take the horse to his stall and return immediately.

SAMBO. *(Carefully folding cloak.)* Yes, sah; yes, sah. Dar's a man——

BURR. Well—why don't you do as I bid you?

SAMBO. Yes, sah—yes, sah; I was jist gwine to tell you 'bout de man—— ·

BURR. *(Impatiently snatches hat and cloak and throws them on arm-chair R.)* Get out, you jabbering old idiot. *(Sambo to L.)*

SAMBO Gwine, sah—gwine, sah. *(Aside.)* Somethin's gwine wrong in dis yer house, shua.

(Exit hastily L.)

BURR. *(Solus.)* At last—at last is the dazzling dream of my life on the verge of realization! Already the sceptre and the crown seem to me but the baubles wherewith to awe the crowd of gabbling fools, and I find myself among the monarchs of this puny earth, regretting, Alexander-like, that there remain no obstacles to overturn. And, yet, a strange misgiving seizes me at times, I know not why nor how, but the pale face of Hamilton ever and again obtrudes upon my thought like an evil dream that will not be dispelled, bringing with it a horrible presentment of evil, link-ing, in some occult way, his fate with mine. What would I not give, could I blot from the canvas of my brain the scene of that morning! Will the picture never fade! Bah! I'll have no more of it. I have far weightier matters to attend to. *(Rings bell.)* Why should I maunder like an old woman, when the southwest is all aglow with the sunburst of my bold enterprise, and the empire of the new world bursts into brilliant being, paling the stars upon our flag.

(Enter Sambo L.)

SAMBO. Did you ring, Mas' Aaron?

BURR. Yes.

SAMBO. An' ye want to know 'bout dat mat' dat——

BURR. I expect some gentlemen here presently. When they come, show them here and see that we are not disturbed.

SAMBO. Yes, sah. Well, as I was a telling you 'bout dat man—

BURR. Pack my trunk ; we will start for New Orleans to-night.

SAMBO Lor'—you gwine away so sudden, an' wid dis old nig-, gah 'long too? Humph ! Well, I see de man a'clombing——

BURR. That's all—you may go.

SAMBO (*In desperation.*) He gwine to tief somethin' shua, ——

BURR. What are you jabbering about ?

SAMBO. 'Bout de one-armed man dat clomb ober de garden wall——

BURR. (*Starting up)* A one-armed man upon my grounds. When did you see him ?

SAMBO. Jest 'fore you come in, sah—he clomb ober de garden wall an'——

BURR. Have the grounds searched at once and thoroughly. If you can find the man, bring him to me by force if need be.

SAMBO. Oh, I'll fetch him. Dis niggah aint no fool niggah ; I's cute. Ef he don't want to come, bring him anyhow?

BURR. I said so. Lose not a moment

SAMBO. (*Performs antics of punching an imaginary head.*) You jest lef it to me — I'll fetch him.

(Exit L.)

BURR. (*Restless and concerned.*) He here ! He is my baneful shadow. Oh, why did I not kill him when I cut him down ! He pursues me with the tenacious hatred of a demon. Who, or what he is I have been unable to ascertain ; but that he is in some way identified with my destiny I have dreadful reason to apprehend. Hatred begets hatred, and that wretch, who has twice sought my life, I hate with all my fiery nature—and yet I fear him, too. Bah, why should I? What a fool I am—a child, when I should be a giant.

(*Enter Sambo L.*) ·

Burr. Well, have you found him?

Sambo. No, sah, not yet; aint see him yet—but de gemmen you expected is here, sah——

Burr. Show them in.

Sambo. Yes, sah.

(*Exit L.*)

Burr Now has the hour come when I must show my mastery of meaner natures, if ever I have mastered in my life. Wilkinson, to me, is a plebeian cur, too vain to lead, too ambitious to trust, too weak to fear, and yet a useful tool if used with skill. His interest once secured in my behalf, the army's mine, and the pet scheme of my life will be a realization so grand, so daring, so unparalleled in modern times, that the world shall reverence with respectful awe the name of Aaron Burr!

(*Sits R. Hastily picks up book of poetry and appears intent thereon as Sambo enters L, preceding Baron Bastrop, Dr. Bollman and General Wilkinson.*)

Burr. Ah, gentlemen—quoting the immortal bard—"You come most timely upon the hour."

Bast. It was nearly a toss-up vedder I come at all. Wasn't it, Doctor?

Boll. Indeed, yes; but for the Baron's admirable horsemanship there would undoubtedly have been a toss up, in which the Baron would have played a very active part. You see, Colonel, we encountered a ghost as we entered your grounds——

Sambo. (*At back, at window L. Shows signs of apprehension. Aside.*) Oh, Lor' I hope he go 'way from here.

Burr. A ghost—I thought the age of ghostly perambulations had passed away.

Gen. Not at all, as the Baron will testify——

Bast. I swear I saw a one-armed man jump across my horse's nose. My horse see him, too, and rear, but dese gentlemen say no—it was but a ghost—and, of course, dey know de country better dan I do—so ghost we'll have him.

S AMBO. (*Aside.*) Yah, yah! I 'spect I's like to cotch dat ghost. (*With air of disgust.*) He aint no ghost.

BURR. (*Concerned.*) A one-armed man, did you say? (*Recovering.*) Ha, ha! Baron, we'll drain a glass to the ghost's health. Sambo, some glasses!

BAST. Good—j'ai tres froid—pardon, gentlemen, I must speak in de French ven I get——

BOLL. Like the pig, Paron?

BAST. How's dat?

BOLL. Stuck!

BAST. Yah, yah, mein herr, ven I get like de stuck pig, and forget de English word.

BURR. Gentlemen, allow me. (*Fills glasses.*) Permit me to propose the health of the most valiant soldier and polished gentleman within the Republic—General Wilkinson——

BOLL. General Wilkinson and the Empire!

BAST. General Wilkinson and de ghost!

GEN. The compliment is so palpably unmerited, my friends, that I fear you jest at me. However, I drink heartily to the new country, and may glory ever follow the bold——

BAST. And may de ghost ever pursue de wicked coward!

BURR. (*Facing window at this moment, sees a face (Nemo's) appear for an instant. No one else sees it. He turns quickly and glances at picture of Hamilton. Starts—trembles—spills wine.*) Great God! How like!

OMNES. What's the matter?

BURR. Did you not see that face? (*Points to window.*)

GEN. I did not.

BOLL. Nor I. You are ill, perhaps.

BAST. Der diefel! Mebbe he was the ghost. Ha! ha!

BURR. (*Recovering himself*) Pshaw! What fools we are to allow a thought to ruffle our composure. But come, gentlemen, we forget our toast—General Wilkinson and the new empire! (*They drink in silence, as though a gloom had fallen on them.*)

SAMBO. (*At back. Aside.*) I guess dis ole coon is gwine to ketch de fox dis time. (*Darts out L.*)

BURR. Now to the object of our meeting. (*Draws forward table upon which are legal documents, pens, ink, etc.*) Naturally, you wish to learn the staunchness of your boat ere you push out into the stream. You shall be fully satisfied. Here are the grants of our territory upon the border—quite enough to found our colony and to await the proper time for conquest. This tract belongs to me. Then, our worthy coadjutor, Daniel Clark, controls the deeds of half the land New Orleans stands on, all of which he has embarked with us, while Blennerhasset, the Prince of the Ohio, throws all his wealth and influence in the scale, and the entire west and southwest are aglow and eagerly await the word to follow our banner. And here—— (*Searches among papers.*)

BOLL. May I assist you, Colonel?

BURR. Thank you, no. I have the details of this business at my fingers'.ends. (*Selects folded map, spreads it open over back of chair—an exaggerated colored drawing.*) And here you see the work of our engineers and surveyors, with notes and figures by our trusty ambassador, Daniel Clark, taken upon the ground

BAST. I should tink so—by a poetic artist, in crayon. De amber predominate, like an impending cloud which is soon to burst and show de sun. Plenty of yellow, which indicates its wealth in gold, and some red—de blood of de enemies of our scheme. How you like de picture? Ha! ha! ha!

BOLL. Baron, I'd no idea you were a man of so much fancy.

GEN. (*Looking at map.*) The artist has omitted the green, the fertility of the land, without which 'twould be a sterile prize.

BURR. There is nothing to apprehend on that score. By this drawing, we will perceive how readily an army might be led into the very heart of the land of promise. To raise that army would be the work of but a single word. Like magic, it would spring into being. But that word cannot be spoken until we are assured of the friendliness of the Republic, that may be secured in one way—the influence of the army. General Wilkinson, you will understand now why I wish you to favor us.

GEN. In case of ultimate success, what then ?

BURR The services of so valuable an officer will merit and command a high reward.

GEN. I may remain inactive—?

BURR. Till the moment comes to strike—

GEN. Then ?

BURR. You are a soldier, and will know what to do. May we rely upon your friendship?

GEN. (*Deliberately and decisively.*) Yes.

BURR. At the proper time, then, I will send you a letter in cipher by the hands of Blennerhasset himself, who will also furnish you the key. It is from his island the expedition will start.

GEN. I shall exact from you, gentlemen, the profoundest secresy regarding my visit here My name must not be mentioned in connection with your project. I am to be the dark horse—

BURR. That carries us to victory. So be it.

BOLL. More work and less talk is my motto. You may rely on me.

BAST. Dat is de correct principle, if dat terminates our pissness (*hesitating for word*), I tink I am a stuck pig again.

BURR. Ha ha ! I understand, allow me to help you out (*places glasses, etc.*) One needs a glass, Baron, to see some things with.

GEN. This time let me propose the sentiment. The new Empire—new rulers and new morals ! (*They drink*)

(*Enter Sambo L.*)

SAMBO. (*Going up to Burr.*) Mas' Aaron, a lady want to see you, I tole her you was engaged, but she say its 'tickler business.

BAST. A lady—ahem ! Oh, we're going——

BOLL. First exemplifier of *new morals.*

GEN. Well, Colonel, we will leave you to your pleasanter duties. I shall await your letter with impatience.

BURR. You shall not wait long. Gentlemen, I thank you for your visit. Sambo, are the horses ready ?

SAMBO. Yes, sah, dey's all ready, I'll bring 'um to de door.

(*Exit.*)

BAST. Au revoir, mon cher Colonel.

BOLL. Is she young and pretty? Ha, ha, ha! well my blessings are yours. (*Exit with Bast.*)

BURR. (*Stopping Wilkinson.*) I rely upon you not only for inaction but assistance ; am I right? (*Searchingly.*)

GEN I do no half-way service—I am with you to the end. (*Exit L.*)

BURR. (*Solus C.*) Then the dream is a dream no more, but a reality, so brilliant in its great achievement that even I am dazzled by its grandeur. And yet, I know not why, in the very ecstasy of my delight, a strange misgiving casts a shadow o'er my hopes, till I almost doubt my own supremacy. Bastrop was right—it was a ghost, and one that will not down ; but what mysterious link there is between his pallid face and *that* (*looking at Hamilton's picture*) and my life, I cannot tell. (*Sits R. The lights begin to lower, representing the gleaming of twilight.*) How pebbles trip us while we scale the mountain peak. Pshaw! I have grown a girl. I will dismiss this idle phantasy. I'll think of Alice, fairest of fair flowers and a peerless queen. She shall indeed be queen and reign with me o'er my new empire.

(*Enter Margaret, L., dressed à la Maud Müller. She steals softly up behind Burr. Crosses at back.*)

Her smile shall be the solace of my life, and her dear heart shall keep forever fresh the kindlier impulses of my nature. Ah, that I were sure she loves me as tenderly, as earnestly as I love her——

MARGARET. (*Affectionately putting her arms about his neck.*) She does, dearest.

BURR. (*Starting up.*) Margaret! You here? I did not speak of you!

MAR. Not of me? Words of love—and not of me? Oh, do not tell me that—say 'twas I you meant. (*Burr paces up and down and across to L. (.*) Do not—do not break my heart! (*Falls on her knees, with face in hands, sobbing. R. C.*)

BURR. (*Aside.*) She has heard too much. I must pacify her. (*Raises her.*) Yes, dear one, I did mean you. But what brings you here, contrary to our compact? (*R. C.*)

MAR. I thank you for that assurance. I knew you could not love another than myself—but when I heard you say so it seemed as if, in that instant, a black cloud had shut the light out of my life ; but now the sun shines again (*nestling*), for I know you were but jesting with me. Tell me you were jesting——

BURR. Certainly – but you have not answered me. Why are you here?

MAR. I could not stay away from you any longer. Do not be angry with me. The days of your absence hang so heavily on me ; and then, when I heard that you were going away and might be gone so long, I could remain no longer——

BURR. Who told you I was going away?

MAR. You did—didn't you?

BURR. I? No. Why do you ask that?

MAR. Because I received a note at my lodging saying that Colonel Burr was going away, and it had no name to it, and you know all your letters to me are written that way, so that I thought it was from you, especially as a pretty bunch of flowers came with it ; I've kissed it ever so many times.

BURR. (*Aside.*) So, evidently, I have a rival ; so much the better. (*Aloud.*) The flowers were not from me.

MAR. (*Gleefully.*) Then you are not going away, Oh ! I am so glad.

BURR. Yes, Margaret, I am going away ; I am a soldier and must go when and where my duty calls me. But, tut child, you should learn to bear separation bravely.

MAR. A soldier's sweetheart should be near him always in the hour of danger. Let me go with you?

BURR. Impossible, you would be in danger.

MAR. There could be no danger where you are, and if there should be, how sweet, how sweet to share that danger with you. Let me go ! (*Coaxing.*)

BURR. Undoubtedly, fair mistress, we shall have ladies in our train. I must order coaches and luxuries and toilet-tables. The ammunition wagons shall carry face-powder. To be sure you shall go, dear Margaret.

Mar. (*Bursting into tears.*) Do not trifle with me. It is the one wish of my life to be with you always, in safety and in danger. I would be your slave. Kill me if you will, and I will kiss the hand that strikes the blow; but do not play with my poor bursting heart as if it were a bauble of no value. Please take me with you, Aaron. I conjure you by the inspiration of the burning words of love you have whispered in my ear, to take me with you.

Burr. (*Moodily.*) It is absurd—it is preposterous—

Mar. If you do not, I cannot live. I cannot abide away from you. Take me, and none shall know that I am with you.

Burr. Indeed! And how would we accomplish that?

Mar. Have you never heard of women in a camp, disguised as soldiers? I would go as aide-de-camp—as orderly—or what you will, so that my duties were near you.

Burr. This is the very ecstasy of folly. I fear, sweet one, that such habiliments as you propose would scarcely suit that charming figure.

Mar. (*Smiling through her tears.*) Nay! I have tried the experiment; and I make so spruce a lad that you could not help being proud of me. See! (*She takes Burr's cloak and hat from chair and puts them on jauntily and parades before mirror near window—makes salute, etc.—pistol shot, crash of mirror—Nemo appears at window, having fired and mistaken Margaret for Burr.*)

Mar. (*Screams.*) My God, what's that! (*Turns and catches glimpse of Nemo at window with gesture of terror—falls and is caught by Burr.*)

Burr. Help! bring lights here quick! speak, Margaret; I have been cruel, heartless to you, speak to me!

(*Sambo and other servants enter with lights.*)

Mar. I am not injured.

Burr. Thank heaven for that.

Mar. (*Coyly.*) May I go with you?

Burr. Yes, sweet one.

QUICK CURTAIN.

ACT II.

SCENE I.

Garden of the Blennerhasset manor by moonlight. House and piazza practically opening into garden. Set shrubbery and trees, rustic seats, etc. Mr. and Mrs. Blennerhasset enter from house, L.

MRS. B. My dear, you seem agitated and wearied. You are not well, but your illness is more of the mind than of the body. What is it? Let your wife share your thoughts and your troubles, as she does your happiness.

BL. The happiness with which you dower me, for were it not for you I should be a pauper in regard to happiness.

MRS. B. You entrusted me the other night with the secret of some great enterprise in which you were about to engage——

BL. Nay! Not so, precisely—of one in which I was tempted to engage.

MRS. B. And with Colonel Burr.

BL. Yes; with that mysterious friend and gifted man, who is bound, I am sure, to succeed in all he undertakes.

MRS. B. Then why not embark with him? I will not be jealous, for I shall share your glory. Shall I not?

(*He draws her toward him affectionately.*)

BL. It would not be glory if you shared it not.

MRS. B. Come now, Harman, we have been married too long for such pretty speeches.

BL. But I am one of those who believe that the successful husband is he who always plays the *rôle* of lover.

MRS. B. Of course, Harman, you mean to his own wife?

BL. In this instance, being so divinely blessed, I could not mean otherwise.

MRS. B. That is real charming. But come, now, tell me why you are so depressed and restless.

BL. But a moment ago I told you that I was strangely tempted to join Colonel Burr in his daring, dazzling scheme. I now tell you that I have *done* so—I am committed to it!

MRS. B. I see nothing so horrible in all this.

BL. But I have misgivings—strange forebodings. I feel as if my friends had all deserted me.

MRS. B. (*Putting her hand over his mouth.*) Ah, Harman, where am I?

BL. You are more than friend. Shall I tell you a dream I had this evening while sleeping in my library?

MRS. B. Do.

BL. You will call me foolish ; but it seemed to me while I slept that you and our two loved ones were in a fairy shallop, dancing upon the bright waters of a silver lake. Presently the rippling waves began to swell, and the fair sky above became overcast ; then a shattered boat neared us, having within it a single rower, and he begged to be admitted into our vessel. As we granted his request the storm increased to a tempest, and from a tempest to a tornado ; but above the roar of the maddened elements rose a clear, fiendish laugh as of exultation ; when, turning, we beheld the stranger in our bark had taken the helm, and was pointing us out into the midst of the blackened lake ! Lo ! there, on its opposite shore, had arisen an edifice more magnificent than any I had ever yet imagined ! It was a palace, set with many-colored brilliants. on whose lofty dome, surmounting all, blazed a red, fiery, fascinating meteor. As we gazed, enraptured, a thunderbolt—so fierce, it seemed to shatter the universal vault of heaven ; prostrating all, it swept the brilliant structure down into the seething waters of our darkling lake ; then, amidst the blackness of eternal despair, I started from my sleep

MRS. B. Ah, Harman, Harman ! I do not wonder you were deeply moved.

BL. Nor was that all : as we sank below the swirling waters, our helmsman, assuming a demon's guise, flapped his raven wings

and disappeared with a hideous laugh. It seemed to me pro-
phetic.

MRS. B. Tut, tut! 'twas but a sleeping fancy after all—dismiss
it.

(*Enter Alice from house, L.*)

See, here shines a star upon our haven which should dispel
such gloomy meditations. Come Alice, dearest, your uncle here
is dull, can you not cheer him with a song?

ALICE. Why, uncle, fie! you should leave long faces and despondency to love-sick girls, whose lovers are untrue—Ha, ha, ha!
why, look at me, I am never sad.

BL. Then I presume you are not a love-sick girl.

ALICE. Ah! yes I am (*facetiously sighing,*) but, ha, ha, ha!
my lover is truth itself.

BL. You have excellent spirits my dear girl; but come, the
song.

ALICE. If you insist.

SONG.

FOND HEARTS MUST BREAK.

Melody—"HAPPY MOMENTS."

I'll tell a tale of love to thee,
As old as tale by minstrel told,
'Tis of a maiden fair to see,
Who loved a knight both strong and bold.
He breathed to her the lovers' vow,
In words that burned as Hecla's breast;
And on her blushing cheek and brow
Impassioned kisses hotly pressed.

The maid believed, as maids will do,
In spite of precept old as pain;
Her lover was all truth, she knew,
To doubt would let no joy remain.
With tears of mingled grief and pride,
She saw her loved one ride away,
Soon to return to claim his bride,
And make amends for love's delay.

3

To stranger climes the knight did rove,
Nor came he back to claim his bride ;
He breathed the self-same tale of love,
In many a listening ear beside.
The maiden watched through weary years,
The faithless loved one's fond return ;
But ne'er came balm to stay the tears,
Nor soothe the breaking heart's concern.

Ah, gentle maiden, cease to grieve—
Nor let thy bitter anguish grow ;
For ever while love's lips deceive,
Fond hearts must break and tears must flow.
Thy lover may not come again,
Yet is the sky as bright and blue ;
Birds still their sweetest carols sing,
And other loves will come to woo.

——o——

BL.   Alice, when you were home last year, did Colonel Burr
not visit your father's house?

ALICE.   He did, frequently.

BL.   And you saw him ?

ALICE.   (*Looking away.*) I had that honor.

BL.   What do you think of him ?

ALICE.   (*Confusedly.*) Why—why do you ask ?

MRS. B.   Do not be alarmed, dear ; he means, how do you regard him as a general—a soldier?

ALICE.   (*Coyly.*) I should say, he were born to make conquests.

MRS. B.   Indeed !   And has our Alice suffered from the soldier's skill ?

ALICE.   (*Still more confused.*) Of course, I mean conquests on
the battle-field.

MRS. B.   (*Stroking her hair.*) Certainly, my darling, young
girls always mean such conquests when speaking of handsome
colonels.

(*Enter Sambo, staggering under travelling bag, etc.*)

SAM.   Is this yeah house the place whar Massa Blummerhasset
libs ?

BL.   I am Mr. Blennerhasset.

SAM. Oh, you is Mas' Blummerhasset? Your sarvint (*bows.*) I's glad to see you, shuah!

BL. You are evidently the forerunner of some one.

SAM. No, I's not; I's Sam, dat's all, and I's loss my tref, and I's mighty tired, shuah (*sits on bag.*)

BL. But you came from some one?

SAM. You're right thar, sartin shuah. The preacher man down at our plantation said dat all us niggers come from—from—no, it wasn't pork—come from—

ALICE. Ham?

SAM. You're right, Missy; that's it.

BL. But who is your master? Whose luggage is that?

SAM. My massa, sah, is de Colonel; and dis is de Colonel's nigger, sitting on de Colonel's luggage; and mighty glad to sit dar, too. I tell you now, dat's so, honeys.

ALICE. ⎫
MRS. B. ⎬ What Colonel?
BL. ⎭

SAM. Why, mas' Colonel Burr! Is dar any more Colonels anywhar?

BL. Why didn't you tell us?

SAM. Why didn't you ask me? I'll tell you ebberyting. I's de most obliginest nigger in de whole worl'. But here he comes hisself now.

(Enter Colonel Burr, in military cloak, hat, etc.)

BL. (*Aside.*) His face recalls my vision. His were the very features of our demon pilot.

ALICE. (*Aside.*) Aaron! How my heart throbs! I am so happy!

BURR. I wish you good evening, my noble friend; and you, madame, worthy wife of so worthy a man. What! the fair Alice, too! This is pleasure past belief.

MRS. BL. You are right welcome, Colonel Burr, to our secluded home; the more so as my husband tells me you are soon to leave our country for a home in the Southwest.

BURR. Not without my very dear friends, I hope.

BL.   No, not without us.   We shall be your companions in the new settlement.   But permit us to see to your comfort, Colonel.   Come, my dear.   Follow us, Sam.

(Exit into house, R.)

SAM.   Yes, massa, I's right wif you, shuah!   *(Aside.)*   All 'long dis nigger been want to get to de kitchen.

(Exit, following Blenn., R.)

MRS. BL.   You will excuse us, Colonel, for a short time, I know.   I presume Alice can take care of you in our absence.

ALICE.   Maybe not; 1 am told soldiers are hard to manage.

BURR.   They should not be, since they are the best disciplined of all men.

MRS. B.   Be careful that your present deportment proves it.

(Exit, following Blenn. R.)

BURR.   *(L. C.)*   Alice, to what bountiful good fortune do I owe this happiness?

ALICE.   *(R. C.)*   I knew you were coming here.   Oh, I know something of your plans.

BURR.   Indeed!   You flatter me by taking such an interest in my welfare.   Pray, what do you know of them?

ALICE.   You are going to be an emperor, or something like that.

BURR.   Not so magnificent, perhaps, but yet I anticipate a grand achievement.   Do you wish that I should succeed?

ALICE.   *(Somewhat sadly.)*   Certainly, I do—but is not ambition a dangerous trade?

BURR.   Only to him who falters.   The men who grow dizzy while climbing are those who fall.   One must look constantly aloft.

ALICE.   And then one forgets constantly those they have left below.

BURR.   One never forgets those he would have bask with him in the glory above.

ALICE.   *(Naively.)*   What do you mean, Colonel?

BURR.   We are not yet in the field.   Military titles are out of place.

ALICE. Then, what do you mean, Aaron?

BURR. (*Taking the hand of Alice.*) Need I tell you again how devotedly I love you?

ALICE. Deceiver! To how many have you professed the same?

BURR. To hundreds, if you will, but to only one with sincerity and truth. I look into her eyes now.

ALICE. I fear you; you are wedded to the army.

BURR. Cannot Mars bask in the stellar radiance of Venus?

ALICE. I cannot tell you; as I understand astronomy, it is not a sentimental science.

BURR. Alice, give me some assurance that my devotion is not at least unwelcome.

ALICE. Forgive me if I wrong you, by even for an instant doubting your sincerity, but by your own admission you have professed love for many, may not I but swell that list of idle protestations.

BURR. Sweet one, by all my hopes of worldly honor, I swear—

ALICE. Hush, 'tis out of fashion now to love by oaths, but as you love me, will you avow it openly?

BURR. I will; I would at once declare my love for you to all the world did not circumstances forbid me. Trust me, believe me, Alice, and ere long I shall return to you as the richest treasure of my life—to halo you with a new found glory. There is a glorious destiny awaiting me; it shall be laid at thy feet as the guerdon of thy slave.

ALICE. You fascinate me, and yet you frighten me. Why delay? Why concealment? It is a strange wooing that shrinks avowal.

BURR. I grant you; but to woo a princess one needs be politic.

ALICE. You forget, there are none such in this democratic land.

BURR. Thou will be, and you shall be the first. Will you not consent to share with me the glory of my conquest?

(*A pause. Nemo appears behind shrubbery. Starts at seeing Burr.*)

NEMO. (*Aside.*) Ha! ha! my wily Colonel, I've tracked you well.

Burr. Your answer, dearest one.

Alice. Not now—not now. My heart had plead and won your cause ere you had breathed a word of love to me. And yet—no, no—I must leave you.

(*Nemo rustles bushes accidentally and dodges out of sight.*)

Alice. What's that? (*They listen.*)

Burr. 'Twas nothing. Your silence is an agony of doubt. Say you are mine——

Alice. No, no, no, no. Here comes my uncle. He must not see my agitation. (*Breaking away from him.*)

Burr. (*Detaining her.*) Say you will give me your answer here when all the house is still.

Alice. You must not ask me to.

Burr. I shall be here awaiting you.

Alice. You will await in vain. I will not come. Good-night.

Burr. (*Hastily kisses her.*) I shall be here !

Nemo. (*Aside.*) And so shall I, false wooer.

(*Exit Alice hastily behind piazza R. as Blenn. enters R. from house.*)

Bl. My very dear friend, you must be tired. Come, have a glass of wine, and then to bed—but where is Alice ?

Burr. She bade me good-night but a moment ago and left me to my meditations and the moon. It's a lovely night. Come, before we seek our rest, let me deliver the business which called me here.

Bl. With all my heart. Proceed. Has General Wilkinson promised his assistance ?

Burr. He has, and all is now ready except the marshaling of our forces For that there must be a convenient rendezvous.

Bl. Why not use my island here ? 'Tis at your disposal.

Burr. The best place in the world ; though, my dear friend, I should not have presumed so mnch on your generosity as to suggest it.

Bl. There must be no delicacy now. I am launched with you upon this enterprise, and what is mine is yours.

Burr. (*Grasping his hand.*) Thanks, my very dear friend. I shall never forget your kindness. The flotilla is already built, and lies some thirty miles above here. At the proper moment we can leave here, and with our men and stores quietly drop down the river to Vick's landing, where Wilkinson will be ready to welcome and to join us. I shall at that time be in New Orleans, so that this expedition will be yours to command. (*Nemo seen at back.*)

BL. Indeed, you place more confidence in me than my poor abilities merit.

BURR. Confidence should meet with confidence. I will send you full instructions how to act, and inclose also a letter to General Wilkinson, which I shall intrust to your special care. On no account let it leave your hands; for though it will be in cipher, its contents will bear gravely on our scheme. (*Nemo listening to all this.*) To avoid a chance mistake, my messenger will wear a sprig of ivy round his hat, and will answer only to the words "the southwest wind." Will you remember them?

BL. I shall remember.

NEMO. (*At back, aside.*) And I shall not forget.

BL. Will my instructions be likewise in cipher?

BURR. They will, the same as Wilkinson's. This package (*handing small package*) contains the key which, with a little attention and practice, will readily make the cipher plain to you.

BL. God grant we may be entirely successful. But——

BURR. There is no "*but;*" we *cannot* fail. Come, let me trespass on your hospitality and get to bed; I'm much fatigued.

BL. You are more sanguine of success than I. A weight oppresses me.

BURR. Then cast it off, and think no more of it. It is too late to retreat. It is dangerous to go back. It is glorious to go ahead.

(*They re-enter the house, R.*)

NEMO. (*Advancing cautiously, C.*) Has Heaven no retribution left to smite that man—that heartless, sweet-tongued hypocrite—that lying, bragging, scheming knave, whose soul's more black than deep perdition's self; who bears within the outward form of man the villainies and instincts of a devil—that——? But, no; I will not spend my breath in idle oaths while there is work to do. Rest, rest in fancied peace, my fangless, pretty cur, and sleep, and dream of a sceptre that is all but won, and see it dashed from your hand just as your gloating fingers close about it, by the poor worm that grovels in the dust and yet can sting! "The southwest wind" I shall remember; fear not. But, hush! Who is this approaching? A man. 'Tis he! and alone! Thank God! (*Makes significant movement for pistol.*) No; I am deceived; 'tis another—a stranger. (*Conceals himself as before.*)

(*Enter Margaret, R. 1st, dressed as soldier, with long overcoat, etc.*)

MAR. I am so weary. (*Throws herself upon seat.*) I have followed close upon him, and here I am told I may meet him. He said that I might go with him, but he could not wait for me, and so I followed him. He would have waited if he could, I know, for he loves me—I'm sure he does; for did he not tell me so in words so sweet that I could dwell forever in their sound and drink their music to my soul till I should die of too much ecstasy. 'Tis late; I must knock and ask for him. How overjoyed he'll be to see his faithful Margaret in this vast wilderness, and I shall rest once more upon his breast. Oh, joy, joy, how eagerly I meet my love! I will knock.

(*Is going toward house as Alice appears in wrap. Margaret shrinks back in shadow.*)

ALICE. I cannot rest. I said I would not come, but my recreant heart gainsays my tongue, and, as the obedient needle to the loadstone draws, so am I drawn against my reason and my will to meet him here.

MAR. (*L. Aside.*) A female figure! I am glad of that; I will speak to her. (*Comes out of shadow.*)

ALICE. (*Rushing to Margaret.*) Aaron! My love!

MAR. (*Starting back. Aside.*) Aaron! My love! Do I hear aright?

ALICE. Do you not wish to hear my answer?

MAR. (*Choking.*) Yes.

ALICE. Be not cold to me. I will be your bride— (*Margaret screams and staggers back.*) What is this? (*Seizes Margaret's* *wrist and looks into her face.*) A woman, and in this guise ! What do you here? * Speak, or I shall alarm the house !

MAR. Colonel Burr——

ALICE. What of him ? Why do you seek him?

MAR. He is in that house? (*faintly.*)

ALICE. Well ?

MAR. He expects me ; I am his——

ALICE. You are his what ?

MAR. In the sight of Heaven I am his——

ALICE. Go on ; go on. His— -

MAR. Wife !

ALICE. 'Tis false !

MAR. He loves me tenderly.

ALICE. (*C.*) 'Tis false again, poor, miserable creature ! Do you dream that he would stoop so low as to consort with your kind? His soul is great and noble, and is incapable of duplicity.

MAR. (*L. C.*) You love him ! you dare to love him ! You *shall* not ! No, no, no (falling on her knees); do not love him ! Spare me—he is all I have in this wide world ; and if I lose him, life will be so black a void that hell itself will have no torture like it.

ALICE. Poor wretch ! I hate you for those words, and yet I pity you. He never loved you.

MAR. Ah yes, he did, and does still. He has sworn it but recently, in accents so tender and so true that to doubt would be a sacrilege against all honesty and virtue.

ALICE. Miserable creature, what you say is false ! Were you to swear it a thousand times, it would not weigh against his sim_ ple word.

NEMO. (*Coming forward, C.*) What she has said is true. (*Alice and Margaret both start.*)

MAR. (*L., facing Nemo.*) My God ! Leave me ! leave me ! Your presence tortures me beyond endurance. (*Sinks on knees and buries face.*)

ALICE. (*R.*) Who are you? I see it all : you are here together for some evil purpose. I'll give the alarm. (*Burr appears from house, R. Alice rushes to him.*) Who are these strange people? Send them away. They have asked for you.

BURR. (*Advancing to crouching figure of Margaret. Nemo is a little out of sight, behind tree, L.*) For me? Do you wish to see me?

MAR. (*Raising her head.*) That voice is his! (*Springing up and rushing to him.*) Ah, Aaron, my love! my life! I am here! (*Alice watches them closely.*)

BURR. (*L. C., starting back, hastily takes Margaret's face in his hands, and scrutinizes it.*) Margaret! Silly fool, begone. (*Casts her roughly off. She falls to the ground.*)

ALICE. (*R., to Burr, earnestly.*) Who is that woman?

BURR. I do not know.

ALICE. You do. She knows you. She loves you. I demand to know the truth.

BURR. A poor young girl, whose life I once saved.

ALICE. And you never loved her?

BURR. Never. I have never seen her since till now.

NEMO. (*Springing forward.*) Perjured villain! you shall die with that lie fresh upon your soul! (*Shoots at Burr. Margaret meanwhile throws herself between. Burr stands erect.*)

MAR. No, no, no, no! he is my love. (*Shot takes effect in Margaret, who reels and falls—Burr catching her.*)

BURR. O God! must it ever be that those who love me shall suffer thus? (*Bending over her, supporting her head.*)

TABLEAU.

CURTAIN.

ACT III.

SCENE I.

*Interior of Farm-house of Zekiel Green, at extremity of the Blen-
nerhassett Island. Zekiel discovered in the act of arraying
himself in a tight-sleeved, long-bodied, pea-green jacket.*

(Enter Patience Green, his aunt, L)

PATIENCE. What on airth air yew a doin', Zekiel Green ? Air
yew gone clean out of your seven senses?

ZEKIEL. Plague take the pesky coat ! What was that you were
a sayin', old gal ?

PATIENCE. (*Bridling.*) Air yew aware, Z. Green, Esq., tew
whom yew air addressin' those words of disrespect?

ZEKIEL. In course I am. I am addressin' them tew my dear
Aunt Patience. (*Gets coat on after burlesque effort, and coming forward, kisses Patience. She bursts into tears, and rocks herself in a
chair, covering her face with her apron.*)

PATIENCE. Oh, your poor dead mother, that is gone ! and
oh, your poor pa, what is dead ! could they have lived to see this
sight here, I reckon it would have broke their hearts. (*Cries
afresh.*)

ZEKIEL. Wal, I guess they'd been willin' to resk the heart
business for the sake of bein' here. But, tarnation snakes ! what
is the matter anyhow?

PATIENCE. Just as if you didn't know !

ZEKIEL. Swear our cows may go dry if I do ! Come, now ;
what is it?

PATIENCE. (*Rising majestically, and pointing.*) Why, you've
gone—and—got—a—new—coat !

ZEKIEL. S'posin' I have ; what then ? It was my set of harness that I sold, and it was my money bought the coat.

PATIENCE. It is not your gay and ungodly attire, Zekiel, that annoys me; you will have to answer for that above. But when your poor dear mother, that is gone, said to me, "Be a mother to Zeke," I said I would.

ZEKIEL. That's because there was nary other chance of being——

PATIENCE. What's that?

ZEKIEL. I said there was no chance of your lettin' up. Go on.

PATIENCE. After all these years, what do I see? A new coat! what does it mean!

ZEKIEL. It means a set of harness.

PATIENCE. So it does mean a set of harness. It means, Zekiel, that yew air goin' tew git married! That's what it means. Yew air a courtin'. (*Overcome by this thought, she throws herself down on chair and weeps.*)

(*Enter Burr, C. fr. L.*)

BURR. Good morning, friends! I hope I haven't disturbed any family discussion?

ZEKIEL. No, sir; it hadn't got as far as a family discussion. Aunt Patience here was only a blowin' about my goin' to get married.

PATIENCE. How can you, Zeke! You air dreadful! (*Aside.*) What a handsome gentleman! Now, if some people only had eyes, there would be some sense in marrying. (*Smooths her apron and manages to take a look in the mirror.*)

BURR. Well, marriage is a very good thing, and is undoubtedly the destiny of every man and woman.

ZEKIEL There now, Aunt Patience, dew yew hear?

BURR. But I come on another errand—one that separates families, instead of uniting them. I come on an errand of war.

PATIENCE. (*Falling back.*) O Lord!

BURR. You may perhaps have heard something of a new military movement toward the Southwest?

ZEKIEL. I have heard of it, sir, and I knew yew when yew came in. Yew air Colonel Burr.

BURR. (*Bows.*) I am the same, and it is about this scheme I want to see you. We need men. (*Looking significantly at Zekiel.*)

ZEKIEL. (*Assuming a strut.*) Did yew say yew needed men ?

BURR. I did.

ZEKIEL. Wal, owin' to malaria and the Injuns, they air rather scarce about here just now ; but, thank heaven, there air some left.

BURR. (*Looking at Zekiel.*) I can easily see there are some fine specimens left.

PATIENCE. (*Looking at Burr, aside.*) And so can I.

BURR. I want to find out, friend Green—for such I understand your name to be—whether you will undertake to manage a recruiting station down here for my forces ?

ZEKIEL. Geerusalem ! but won't I ?

BURR. In case you do, I will make you Captain, and call the Company after you. It shall be Green's Militia.

ZEKIEL. (*Dancing with joy.*) What dew yew think of that, Suky ? Captain Green !

PATIENCE. Yes, and a very green Captain, I swan !

ZEKIEL. Come, now ; that ain't fair. I aint a soldier yet.

BURR. All in good time. Your instructions will be given you.

PATIENCE. Lawkes ! what an honor for you, Zeke ! How proud your poor dear dead and gone——

ZEKIEL. Never yew mind about that now. Why don't you get the breakfast ready ? Mebby Colonel Burr will sit down tew our frugal feast, as I hearn the dominy say ?

PATIENCE. Oh, you will ; wont you, sir ? I kin get it ready in a jiffy. A nice slice of crisp Ohio bacon, sum new lain eggs, sum buckwheat cakes, sum fresh milk, sum maple scrup, some fresh doughnuts, sum——

BURR. Thank you, my dear, good woman, you are as hospitable as you are charming ; but I must return to Mr. Blennerhassett's for breakfast.

PATIENCE. (*Aside.*) Dear, lawkes ! What a nice man. (*Smoothing apron and cap.*) What real good taste he has ! he's none of yer harum-scarum men, who's always running after giddy young girls. But really, *my very dear Colonel Burr*, you *will* have a glass of new milk, just to oblige me, won't you, neow ? (*Insinuatingly.*)

BURR. (*Amused.*) Indeed, you are so pressing, who *could* refuse you ?

PATIENCE. Dear me, I knew you would ! I'll go and fetch it from the dairy. (*Aside.*) What a real nice man !

(*Exit, L.*)

ZEKIEL. (*Coming forward.*) She's a real good soul, but sometimes she's hefty pecooliar. You mustn't mind her, though. The old gal means well.

BURR. Indeed ! I deem her a very pleasant old lady. But I'm glad she has left us alone for a few moments, as I wish to speak to you privately.

ZEKIEL. Wal, that's kind of sing'lar ; but skoot ahead, old mud-skudgeon ! (*Burr checks his familiarity with a glance. Confused.*) I mean Colonel. I'm all ears.

BURR. (*Aside.*) Nearly. You have heard of the attempted murder last night ?

ZEKIEL. What's that ? Murder ? Whar ?

BURR. At Blennerhassett's.

ZEKIEL. Dew tell ! What abeout it ? Let's hear.

BURR. There was a one-armed man concealed in the shrubbery.

ZEKIEL. A one-armed man ? Consarned if I didn't fetch him over in one of my boats !

BURR. And a woman. Did you ferry her, too ?

ZEKIEL. Nary a woman.

BURR. She was in men's clothes—soldier's clothes.

ZEKIEL. The deuce ! That man in soldier's clothes was a woman ! Wal, dem my buttons ! Cuss me if that warn't the reason why he—no, I mean she—no, I mean they—it ?—it wouldn't say a consarned word 'cept yes and no ; and I tried my mightiest tew find out whar he—it came from. Wal, go ahead.

BURR. Well, this one-armed man shot at me while I was talking to the strange woman, and the ball struck her, wounding her severely, though not seriously.

ZEKIEL. And did he get away ?

BURR. Not then. We overtook the ruffian and secured him

in an out-house; but during the night he made his escape, and is now on the island, doubtless. Is there any way for him to get across the river except by the use of your boat?

ZEKIEL. None, unless he swims, an' I guess he'll hardly try that, for the current's pretty swift right about here. We'll ketch him.

BURR. I don't want to catch him. I want him to escape.

ZEKIEL. (*Astounded.*) To escape!

BURR. Yes. I want you to contrive to leave a boat and oars a little up the stream, so that he can steal them and get away. Do you understand? (*Taking out purse significantly.*)

ZEKIEL. Can't say as I do. You see, I don't like—— (*Burr jingles money.*) Wal, I spose as I'm a soldier now I must obey my superior's orders.

BURR. You will find it advantageous. (*Gives purse.*) You must speak to nobody regarding what I have just said to you.

ZEKIEL. I'm dumb as a hedge-fence Hush, here comes Aunt Patience (*looking out*), and there's Miss Alice with her looking as fresh as a primrose.

BURR. (*Aside.*) Alice here? I am sorry for that.

(*Enter Alice and Patience, C. fr. L.*)

ALICE. Ah! Colonel Burr, I see you have anticipated my errand here.

BURR. If it be to warn these good people of that villain's escape and to secure his recapture, I have indeed forestalled you.

ALICE. His escape! Has he too escaped! Did you not undertake to guard him personally?

PATIENCE. Who's escaped? What's that?

ZEKIEL. Don't be curious, Aunt Patience. Come in and get breakfast and I'll tell you about it.

(*Exit Zeke and Patience, L.*)

BURR. I did; but I was so careless in my duty that I let the rascal get away.

ALICE. You a soldier, too—that's very odd. Perhaps not more so though than my own carelessness. My poor wounded bird also has flown away——

BURR. What! Margaret gone!

ALICE. Margaret! How knew you her name?

BURR. Did she not mention it last night? But tell me—has she indeed gone?

ALICE. I watched her all night long; she turned and tossed upon the bed, burning with fever and babbling to herself.

BURR. What did she say?

ALICE. Nothing intelligible—her shoulder, where the ball struck her, pained her greatly, and it seemed to divert her wayward thoughts from the subject of her dreams.

BURR. (*Aside.*) A most fortunate diversion.

ALICE. In her semi-waking moments I questioned her about her errand to you, and (*hanging her head*) of her relationship with you. You must forgive me, Aaron, I am but a woman, and one of those who love but once. I am sure that this girl has loved you, and I do not blame her for that. She could scarce avoid the fate if you crossed her humble path. I rest sweetly contented, however, in the assurance that you love none but me. It is a pleasant dream.

BURR. May you never awake from it, darling.

ALICE. Awake from it! Awake from it! It would be my death or yours; but let us not talk in this wild way. Near dawn I fell asleep, and when I woke she had gone, having donned the dress I had placed beside the bed. I am glad you have taken measures to have the would-be assassin intercepted. When I spoke to Mr. Blennerhasset about having the island searched, he told me that you had volunteered to attend to it—and how about the sick and wounded girl—we must find her.

BURR. All the arrangements have been made. No one can leave the island save by Mr. Green's boats. I have already had a conversation with him.

ALICE. One question more, dearest—and forgive me if it is an iteration: You do not know—at least remember—this girl?

BURR. I do not recall that I have ever seen her since I was fortunate enough to save her life until last night. Doubtless her gratitude misled her.

ALICE. It is enough; I am the happiest of women.

Burr. And I of men.

Alice. And yet, I do not know why I should be so happy when a helpless creature who has loved you—and I do feel heartily sorry for the poor girl, as I said last night, who is now roaming this island sick and wounded.

Burr. I will see that she is found and cared for. Return home, dear Alice, with that assurance. I will follow you as soon as I have spoken with our ferry-man. (*Leads Alice to door.*)

Alice. Do not remain long away.

Burr. I will not, dearest.

(Alice exits, C. to L.)

Burr. (*Solus.*) So far, the cards run well. Fortune favors me. Both have escaped. It suits my purpose well to help them on their way.

(Scene Changes.)

SCENE II.

A woodscape between Blennerhassett's mansion and Green's house.

(Enter Nemo hastily, R. 1st.)

Nemo. (*Solus.*) Still the game goes on, and I, as ever, hold the losing cards. Do I? We shall see—we shall see. It cannot be—it cannot be that villainy shall always hold the trumps. I hate him with all the hatred of a soul that's damned. Why should I not? My destiny is fixed; Heaven has chosen me as its instrument of retribution. How it chafes me to be compelled to fly! And yet I must. But not from him. No, no; not from him! Ah, here comes some one! The lady of last night. Shall I confront her? I will, and warn her of her danger in listening to the fair words of that oily fiend. (*Retires, L. up.*)

(Enter Alice, L. 1st.)

Alice. Would that I were satisfied. If he is true to me, he is my God—I worship him. But were he a thousand times the hero

5

my love would make him, and false to me, I'd curse him with the vehemence of a fiend.

NEMO. (*Coming suddenly forward.*) Then curse him as a thing most damnable.

ALICE. (*Shrinking back.*) Who are you ?

NEMO. Do not fear me, young lady.

ALICE. You are a would be murderer !

NEMO. Are you to judge me without knowing the incentive for my act? He is a villain steeped in crime. I overheard his protestations of love for you ; believe me, fair lady, when I say that he was false to you as to all the world beside, and to warn you of your danger——

ALICE. Can you prove to me the truth of what you say ?

NEMO. I can.

ALICE. And if you do I shall despise him as heartily as you do.

NEMO. And pursue him as I do ?

ALICE. I shall thwart him in his grand aspirations if I can.

NEMO. You promise that !

ALICE. I do ; but I must have some stronger proof than mere suspicion.

NEMO. You shall have convincing proof. First of all, that poor girl, Margaret !

ALICE. Ah ! Margaret, what of her ?

NEMO. What did he tell you of her ?

ALICE. That he had saved her life, and that her gratitude had grown to love ; that he had never met her—never seen her after till last night ; that he never loved her. Was that true ?

NEMO. It was not. Margaret—alas! what shall I say she was to him? Oh, God, it makes me wild to think of it! She was as pure and innocent as you, dear lady, when this villain crossed her path. He met her at her mother's house in New Jersey ; she was then my affianced bride. I loved her as the flowers love the sunshine—as the birds love the free air of heaven ; I loved her so truly that my whole life was bound up in hers, and noon could have no sun more bright than was her sweet smile to me. With his damned insidious arts he won her love away from me, only to ruthlessly destroy the flower he had plucked. I saw her growing coldness and knew the cause of it. A burning, torturing jealousy seized me—Ah, lady, I could not bear to lose that precious thing. Her love——

ALICE. Go on—go on. Did she——

NEMO. One unhappy morning her room was vacant — my pretty bird had flown, and flown off with the hawk. I swore to her poor heart-broken mother I would find them. And I did. I found them in New York. I sought to bring the erring loved one home. Burr sneered at me when I upbraided him. We quarreled. I was unarmed ; but blinded with jealous rage and hate, I struck him to the earth, and seizing the fainting Margaret in my arms, would have borne her off, but that he struck me with his sword, and I lost my arm.

ALICE. Poor fellow ! I am sorry for you.

NEMO. When I was over the weeks of fever I endured I determined to follow him, and take an arm from him as he took mine. It was not till then I learned the secret of my life, and found that my fate was linked with his by a bond of deadly, relentless hatred other than poor Margaret's shame ; and then I swore to kill him.

ALICE. As yet, you have given me no proof. I have but your word ; and I cannot, will not, believe him such a villain.

NEMO. True ; I had forgot How can I prove the truth of what I say ? (*Margaret heard singing, R.*)

Stop ! Is that not she ? How is this ? I thought you had confined her in the house ?

ALICE. She escaped from me this morning. I'm glad I've found her. I can question her.

(*Enter Margaret, dressed in female attire. She is crazed, and in the delirium of fever. Grotesquely arrayed with branches, leaves, etc.*)

MAR. (*Singing*)—

"You are going far away, far away from poor Jeanette,
There's no one left to love me, and you too may forget ;"

Good morning, good people, can you direct me on my way? Here's money for you (*gives branch*)—

ALICE. You are burning with fever, come with me——

MAR. (*Laughing wildly.*) Ha, ha, ha! I know you, you are cunningly disguised—you are the man in the moon. (*Sings.*)

> The man in the moon
> Is a merry old coon,
> A rollicking, frollicking, noisy old fellow,
> Ever happy and glad,
> He never is sad,
> This good-natured, rollicking, frollicking fellow.

Ah! would I were he. I am so unhappy!

ALICE. Poor child. you are——

MAR. (*Peering dreamingly in her face.*) You are beautiful—you stole my love, what did you do with him? (*Looking around and encountering gaze of Nemo, starts and shrinks away.*) Ah! (*then losing herself again—to Nemo.*) You are a good, kind gentleman, to come so far with me, but I can go alone now, thank you.

NEMO. (*Passionately.*) See, see the completeness of his wicked work! This is the flower I nurtured in my heart so tenderly. Margaret, speak to me! Say that you know me!

MAR. (*Weeping.*) He has gone away. Where can I find him? (*Sings.*)

> "Oh, if I were King of France, or, still better, Pope of Rome,
> I'd have no fighting men abroad, no weeping maids at home."

ALICE. Is this not pitiful?

NEMO. Do you ask more proof than this of his villainy?

ALICE. Tell me in what way we can punish him!

NEMO. There is but one way to reach him.

ALICE. What is that?

NEMO. Strike at him through his great scheme. Lay the axe at the tree of his ambition.

> (*Alice walking excitedly up and down.*)

ALICE. But how?

NEMO. He is a traitor to his country, and even now is conspiring to induce the army to desert their flag and march nnder his——   .

ALICE. I cannot believe he is so base!

NEMO. Convince yourself, then. You have access to Blenner-hassett's private papers?

ALICE. Yes—well?

NEMO. Secure, in some way, the key to the correspondence in cypher between Burr and General Wilkinson ; I will attend to the rest.

ALICE. But I cannot stoop——

NEMO. When you are fighting against villains you must not hesitate to use their own weapons against them.

(Margaret, who has been making a wreath, now puts it on and comes down.)

MAR. Come, dear friends, let us hasten away from here. He will think I am not coming. See, there he comes. *(Pointing off, L.)* I knew he would come back. *(Claps her hands.)*

NEMO. It is indeed he. Let us conceal ourselves.

MAR. No; you must fly; he will arrest you.

NEMO. No danger of that ; 'twas he that set me free this morning. Yet I will leave you, as it might not be advantageous to have him see us together. I may speak with you again.

ALICE. Yes ; here, to-morrow. Fly !

NEMO. You will take care of her *(indicating Margaret.)*

ALICE. Yes ; now go.

(Exit Nemo, R 2d. Alice hides herself behind tree, R. 2d, as enter Burr, L. 1st. Margaret runs to meet him. He repulses her and then looks carefully around.)

BURR. You here ! Why did you come to this place to hamper my progress? Foolish, miserable girl, you must return home at once ; your presence here has well nigh ruined me.

MAR. *(L. C.)* Dear Aaron, I did not mean to trouble you, nor to be an obstacle in your path, although I know it leads away from me. I came here because you said I might. Do not chide me, I will be your slave *(Then the insanity returning.)* Won't that be jolly ! I'll be a soldier. Let me be a soldier and ride by your side—— *(Sings.)*

"Let me like a soldier fall."

BURR. You must leave here. Do you understand me?

MAR. (*Sadly.*) Yes; I will leave you if you bid me, though my poor heart is breaking. I am very ill. (*Pressing her hand to her forehead.*)

BURR. No matter, you must leave——

ALICE. (*Aside.*) And this is the man for whom she would sacrifice her life.

MAR. As you say, Aaron. Yes, perhaps your little Margie would only be in the way of your greatness, and she wants to see you a great soldier. You will kiss me once before I go.

BURR. Yes. (*Kisses her coldly.*) There—now go. Follow this path till you arrive at Green's house; he will ferry you across the river. There's money for you. (*Hands money.*)

MAR. (*Shaking her head and declining money.*) No, I want no money, I can walk, I am quite strong again (*staggering, going L.*) My journey will be a short one—a very short one. Good-bye. Think of your little "Margie" sometimes, will you? We'll be friends now, not lovers, and we will laugh when we look back and think how foolish we were to love. Ha, ha, ha! Good-bye— good-bye—(*going, stops—rushes back in paroxysm of grief.*) No, no, no, I cannot, I cannot, I cannot! (*Falls swooning into Burr's arms.*)

ALICE. (*Coming from concealment—excitedly.*) I can endure this no longer. Wretched, cold-hearted man, you stand in your true light.

BURR. (*Aside.*) Alice here! Have you been listening?

ALICE. Chance compelled me to be a witness of your perfidy, and to unmask your treachery.

BURR. You wrong me, Miss Leighton. (*Placing Margaret on grassy bank, R. up.*)

ALICE. If believing you to be a villain wrongs you, then I do. Your cruelty to that poor girl, your duplicity to me, have torn the veil from my eyes, and I behold you, not the hero my dazzled imagination painted you, but a stony demon in the guise of man.

BURR. (*R.*) Have you done?

ALICE. No, I have not done. You have aroused a nature as fiery and as stubborn as your own. I am the daughter of a soldier, Colonel Burr—a soldier, understand ; not a trickster and a traitor. (*Burr flinches slightly.*) You have met your match for once. You have not done well to make an enemy of me. Yes, Margaret (*going to Margaret, R. up, and taking her head in her arms*), your wrongs shall be avenged. We are no longer rivals, but co-workers to destroy the stony image of a blind idolatry, and substitute the light of virtue and of truth.

BURR. (*L. C.*) Miss Leighton, I have listened to your denunciation with inexpressible pain, keener because I think you believe in the truth of what you say. You deem me heartless and cruel. Do you think my heart does not bleed for the sufferings of that poor girl? I would spare her that terrible ordeal if I could ; but there are higher claims upon me. Do not judge me hastily. The lot of genius is to be misconstrued, because misunderstood. The world can no more measure the terrible isolation, the wild yearnings of the ceaseless, consuming passions of its great men than can the placid pool of the forest appreciate the tremendous upheaval of the ocean tempest. It is the penalty of genius that it should sacrifice upon the altar of the world's ignorance all that is noble, generous, and good. Can you wonder, then, that what may seem the extravagance of vice and cruelty may be but the natural outpourings of a soul swayed by impulses more turbulent and resistless than its fellows only because it is grander and more noble. I loved you, Alice, with all the passion of my soul. I never loved that poor child there.

ALICE. Spare yourself the mortification of that confession.

BURR. (*L. C.*) The eagle cannot mate with the dove. He was made for loftier flights, and only occasionally does he come so near the plain. Before I leave you, may I dare to ask if I may hope——

ALICE. Hope! Ay, hope for my life-long detestation! We part, Colonel Burr, as enemies !

BURR. As enemies ?

ALICE. As the bitterest of foes. Go !

BURR. So be it—as foes.

CURTAIN.

ACT IV.

SCENE I.

Interior of Zeke's Farm House, now a recruiting station. Benches, tables, stacks of guns, flags and military paraphernalia scattered about. Recruits, shabbily costumed, playing cards, some reading. Zeke (front) rises from his table, walks with swaggering gesture. He is in burlesque full uniform, with the exception of his coat.

ZEKIEL. (*R.*) Wal, my army's about made up, I reckon, 'cept Sambo and Pat—wont they just make a team! I s'pose I'll have to give Sambo the big drum and make Pat the head cook.

(*Enter Pat and Sambo, C., arm in arm. Sambo has a red coat and Pat a green one. They halt and salute in mock dignity.*)

ZEKIEL. (*R.*) Eyes right! (*Burlesque drill movement.*)

ZEKIEL. First battalion, three paces to the left!

SAMBO. Dat's you, Corporal Pat; you's de first battalion, you is.

PAT. (*R. C.*) Me distinguished friend from Africa, I hev not the honor; I'm the third brigade.

ZEKIEL. (*R.*) Here, you two, do yew hear? I want you to stop ajawin' and mind orders. I'll hev yew in the guard-house for mutiny before long, mind that. Fall in neow and form a hollow square.

(*Sambo and Pat look at each other curiously and then embrace. The lookers-on applaud them. Sambo and Pat exit in military style, C. Enter Nemo, C.*)

NEMO. *L. C.*) Is this the head-quarters?

ZEKIEL. (*R. C.*) Guess so. It might be neow.

NEMO. Is Colonel Burr about?

ZEKIEL. Wal, he might be, and then perhaps he aint. Wont any other soldier do? (*Straightens himself proudly.*)

NEMO. Do not think I made any mistake—the warlike bearing is too evident—you were born for the tented field.

(*Zeke rattles his sword. Fixes neckcloth pompously.*)

ZEKIEL. Want to jine?

NEMO. Yes.

ZEKIEL. Why yes, of course you do. Who wouldn't? What's your name?

NEMO. What's your's, General?

ZEKIEL. (*Aside.*) Great slapjacks, wont that open Patience's eyes—General! (*To Nemo.*) Wal, Colonel, my name is Green.

NEMO. Funny! Why, my name is Green, too.

ZEKIEL. Well, I dew declare, who'd a thought sich a thing. (*Writes down the name and looks at it admiringly.*)

ZEKIEL. Ah, let me see—Was yew any relation to the Greens of——

NEMO. Greenland? No, sir.

ZEKIEL. (*Nettled.*) I didn't say Greenland. Whar was you from?

NEMO. It doesn't matter—I'm a soldier. I come from the wars.

ZEKIEL. All the Greens dew, and some of them are green for dewing it. Now, my dad—Niggerdemus Tophaniah Zekiel was the front of his name—he fit in the wars. Perhaps yew didn't know Niggerdemus Tophaniah Zekiel Green?

NEMO. I had not that pleasure.

ZEKIEL. Ah, he was a soldier; yew always calculated to find him whar the shot was the thickest.

NEMO. Yes——

ZEKIEL. Yes; poor dad, he was thar every time—he drove the ammunition wagon. (*Omnes laugh. Affected.*) He was killed in the war, he was! (*Auditors show signs of repenting their mirth*) He was kicked in the head by a pesky mule. (*Mock grief from all for the death of Zeke's progenitor.*)

Nemo. (*C.*) I like these tales of the battle; they stir my blood as the bugles do. I would like to be in action in the front rank, and as near the General as possible.

Zekiel. Oh, you dew—dew yew? Wal, then you can place yourself there if you've a mind to. I was about to elect an ensign; spose I elect you——

Nemo. Consider me elected.

Zekiel. Good. Now let's shake hands to ratify the bargain—but say, yew haint told me your front name.

Nemo. Ah, true. Well, put it down Nemo.

Zekiel. Well, that's an odd name, young feller, but down she goes.

Nemo. When do you want me to report for duty?

Zekiel. Neow—right neow? If you'll go down to the shanty you'll find sum soldier's fixin's—yew can take the best yew can find. Come right back, 'cause we will drop down the river to-night.

Nemo. I shall be prompt, Colonel. (*Aside, going.*) So, Colonel Burr, you will have a determined soldier in your camp, and one that will follow you to death.

(*Exit, C., Nemo, as the Chaplain, a seedy fellow with a red nose, comes on, C. They encounter. He is made up like a military chadband. The card players break up their games. Two have a dsipute about stakes and draw horse-pistols. Zeke gets hold of the Chaplain and uses him for breastworks while he shouts.*)

Zekiel. Look a-here, yew over there, put them cannon things away. I'll have you court-marshalled. (*Row continues.*) I'll stop your whiskey. (*Instantly the row ceases.*)

Zekiel. (*Very bold.*) I thought that would fetch you.

(*Chaplain trembles.*)

Chaplain. Heaven be praised, there is no gore—no blood · shed. It would be shocking for a soldier in the army of peace to witness violence. Dear me, I am so faint. Now, if we only had a drop of spiritual consolation. (*Soldiers cheer and crowd around.*)

43

SOLDIERS. That's the style! Go on, Captain Green, serve us out something— —

GAMBLER. (*With black eye and hoarse voice.*) Seems to me the winner ought to stand treat, jest out of respect to the church.

CHAPLAIN. Friend, you speak well; I will send you some tracts.

ZEKIEL. Wal, I don't mind. Come now, me brave warriors, dress up, get in line and form yourself into the tin-cup division.

(*Soldiers cheer and fall in rapidly and grotesquely, with much fuss. Green gets into a ridiculously bombastic coat—very gorgeous, huge epaulettes, &c.*)

ZEKIEL. (*Brandishing his sword.*) Now for the refreshments.

(*Enter Patience, C, dressed as a vivandiere, very lean, lanky and funny, a little keg of spirits strung at her side.*)

ZEKIEL. (*Horrified.*) Patience Green, are you aware what your name is and who yew air, and the family yew air disgracin' of— Take them things off——

PATIENCE. (*Bridling.*) I would hev yew to know, Zekiel Green, that I am your survivin' aunt, and that I'm old enough to do as I please. I'm not going to stay here; I'm agoin' with the army—

SOLDIERS. Hurrah!

CHAPLAIN. (*Casts sheep's eyes at Patience and looks lovingly at the cask. Aside.*) How sweet she looks.

PATIENCE. (*Aside.*) There is that handsome preachin' chap; guess those fellows know the marriage service all by heart. (*Sighs.*) Who knows what may happen—Colonel Burr is single!

ZEKIEL. (*Disgusted.*) Old enough to know what yew air doin'. Wal, I should say so. You were old enough for that fifty years ago.

CHAPLAIN. Before we move, gentlemen, I would suggest— ahem—I would mention that, out of compliment to the fair sex, a little hymn or a song, not too secular, would be appropriate.

(*Enter Pat, C.*)

SOLDIER. And there's just the man. Come on, Paddy, a song.

PAL. I dont mind obligin' yez, but me throat's like a turn-pike in July.

(*Patience pours out liquor in cup. Pat drinks and Chaplain passes his hands across his stomach.*

SONG.

Air—"THE JOLLY TAILOR."

Oh, the soldier's life is the life for me,
   To march wid banners flyin';
To blaze wid glory on the field,
   Amid the dead an' dyin'!
Let those who wish it stay at home
   An' die in bed so aisy—
But as for Paddy O'Mahone,
   To die so 'd set him crazy.

        Oh, a soldier's life is the life for me,
          It is so gay and frisky;
        There is lots of fun, wid a sword and gun,
          A scrimmaging for whiskey.

Then he loves the girls, does the soldier true—
   The girls think he's a darlint;
To get a squeeze in warlike arms
   The sweets are always quar'lin'.
A soldier, tho' as bold as Mars,
   Does not fulfil his duty
Unless he's always at the front
   To comfort youth and beauty.

        CHORUS.

And as soon as the fighting is all done,
   He goes back to his widdy,
An' thin he hears the shouts and cheers
   While marching through the city.
His heart beats fast as he goes past,
   An' he feels like all creation,
For he's the idol of the crowd—
   The hero of the nation.

        CHORUS.

Thin och ! what a terrible spree there 'll be,
    As all the boys give welcome.
There's Mike O'Luke and Patsey Duke,
    O'Callahan and Malcome :
The Hagan byes and ould Muldoon,
    And lovely Mother Folger ;
And Mary Ann and all the gang,
    To glorify the soldier.

                  CHORUS.

(*As song ceases fife and drum heard. Enter Sambo, C., beating big drum, and another negro playing fife.*)

ZEKIEL. Ha, the band has arrived ; now for it. Forward ! Right ! March !

(*Zeke keeps time and waves his sword as the crowd, preceded by the musicians, march out. Patience follows waving a flag, and the Chaplain, who takes advantage of the excitement, turns the tap of the cask and catches a drink in his tin cup. He drinks with up-turned eyes and then walks out sanctimoniously. As they disappear, enter Nemo in uniform, C.*)

NEMO. Fools ! They laugh and drink and little dream of what is about to-take place. They have an idea that this fighting life is but a gentle jaunt. I have but one purpose here, and, that fulfilled, I will leave this place forever. (*At window.*) See who comes here—a soldier, and covered with dust. Can it be ? Yes, it is. It is the messenger, the ivy wreathed about his hat. Thank heaven, my plans prosper well.

                  (*Enter Messenger, C. fr. R.*)

MESS. (*R. C.*) Can you direct me, sir, to Mr. Blennerhassett ?

NEMO. (*L. C.*) Quite easily, friend. You have evidently travelled far.

MESS. No, not very. (*Carelessly.*)

NEMO. That's right, that's right ; it were not safe to tell everybody that you have come all the way from Colonel Burr——

MESS. (*Starting.*) How knew you that——

NEMO. (*Laughing.*) By your sprig of ivy and the southwest wind——

MESS. Then you are——

NEMO. Blennerhassett, and you have a letter for me.

MESS. I have two ; the other is for——

NEMO. (*Carelessly.*) For General Wilkinson, which I am to deliver. Am I right?

MESS. You are. (*Takes out letters and hands them to Nemo*) And now, my message delivered, and as a companion waits for me on the other side of the river, I will bid you God-speed and a fair southwest wind.

NEMO. Thank you, my friend, a fair southwest wind (*Exit, C. to R., Messenger—altering his manner*), but not for him. A fierce tornado is brewing, Colonel Burr, which shall forever blast your ambitious schemes and stamp your name with ignominy. This letter to Wilkinson will, I warrant, secure your downfall. We will learn its contents at once. The key to the cypher is in the possession of the lovely Alice, who will glory to aid me to my end. So, so, your most imperial majesty, the owls will soon grow hoarse with hooting at your vain presumption. (*Exit C.*)

SCENE CLOSES.

SCENE II.

Ante-room to ball room at Vick's Landing, near General Wilkinson's headquarters. A hall in first groove in country mansion.

(Enter Wilkinson with letter in hand, R.)

GEN. A letter from Burr at last, and soon Burr himself. By the powers, this plan approaches fruition, and Burr will be an emperor ! We shall see, we shall see. He holds sway now in one place—at least where I envy him—in the heart of the woman I love. Let him look to it, that I do not dethrone him in both particulars. (*Reading letter.*) " Now is the time for you to use your influence. Call upon the army, fire them with ardor, and our grand scheme is a complete success." Ah, Colonel, you little know for whom I am working. Wily, sly, oily knave as you are, you do not dream that you are being fought with your own weapons. I will play with you, my astute Colonel, to the end of your folly—until the empire is a fact, and then I WILL call upon the army, but for what purpose, that remains to be seen.

(*Enter Blennerhassett, L.*)

BL. You have deciphered the letter which I have brought to you?

GEN. Yes ; 'tis not difficult. Both the cypher and the purport is easily comprehended. Burr speaks bluntly.

BL. This is too important a crisis to permit a choice of terms. We must fully understand each other——

GEN. But should the letter have miscarried it might have compromised some of us. Are you quite sure you have kept your key carefully guarded?

BL. Yes ; even my wife, from whom I have few secrets, knows nothing of it.

GEN. Then we are safe.

BL. At this moment we need to be. All is in readiness to strike—the flotilla is even now awaiting our orders. Burr will be here presently. A mistake would be death, shame and disgrace ! The *fête* to-night will be the glittering seal set upon our compact. I hope that it will be as brilliant as I anticipate. Burr is a man who likes a little ostentation. When he is an emperor I suppose the court will outrival in grandeur the temple of the Sun he is so fond of speaking about.

GEN. (*Aside.*) *When* he is an emperor. Now my tastes are simple——

BL. You know the sign we are to wear to show that each heart is true, and to let the others know that all is in readiness for the striking of the blow.

GEN. No. What is it?

BL. Burr, yourself and myself and all those who know definitely the moment of the movement will wear red ribbons in the button hole of the coat. When this is seen the parties to the con—ahem—to the agreement will understand that the clock of fate has struck the glorious hour !

Gen. I am glad you told me. I will be so decorated——

Bl. Do not fail; it would be awkward. The ribbon has another significance, as I learn from Burr. It bids us to assemble at dawn after the ball is over, and formally throw off all allegiance to the United States.

Gen. I will not fail!

Bl. Fail! Without General Wilkinson our empire would be but a dream spun of moonbeams. Till to-night, farewell.

Gen. *(Bowing.)* Till then—— (*Exit Blenn., L.*)

(*Enter Alice, R. Wilkinson puts away letter, to which he has returned, hastily.*)

Alice. (*R.*) Good morning, General. Are you going to the ball?

Gen. (*L.*) Are you?

Alice. Most assuredly.

Gen. Then why ask me? Your being there determines my course.

Alice. (*Archly.*) To stay away of course, I suppose.

Gen. You know differently. To be near you I would absent myself from a battle even ——

Alice. You might have enough of combat and din of war in my society. I am not the most even tempered of women——

Gen. But why should I go to-night? Colonel Burr will be there.

Alice. I hope so.

Gen. You are going to the ball then to see Burr.

Alice. I am, for no other reason.

Gen. He should be a happy man.

Alice. He will be a very unhappy one.

Gen. What do you mean?

Alice. We must be equally frank. How do you regard me?

Gen. I love—I adore you—I——

Alice. (*Coolly.*) That's enough—so does Colonel Burr.

Gen. (*R. C.*) I know it.

Alice. He has proposed for my hand and offers me a seat on the throne he is about to erect.

GEN. And you accepted?

ALICE. Would I not have been foolish to refuse?·

GEN. But suppose he fails—suppose another occupies that throne?

ALICE. He must fail; that throne will never be. Do you understand?

GEN. (*Dazed.*) Hardly. Be more explicit.

ALICE. It is my pleasure, it is my will; in fact, it is my command that the conspiracy be exploded to-night, and that Burr be arrested!

GEN. By whom?

ALICE. By you!

GEN. Impossible—would you have me a traitor to friendship?

ALICE. I know you, General, better than you think I do Your remark a little while ago, about another occupying the throne confirms my suspicions. You mean to betray Burr in the future. Is it less ignoble to be false to a man who would use you for his own selfish aggrandizement than to be a traitor to your country— and you a soldier, too—fie! for shame! Think—at present you are not committed—surrender him to the authorities at once, and you will be applauded for your integrity, fail to do so, and I shall denounce you both, and you will share his fate——

GEN. But what does this mean? Have you and he ——

ALICE. It doesn't matter what has happened. If what you profess as regards myself be true. you should be content to see an estrangement, however brought about.

GEN. I am—I am—but—

ALICE. Then act—the knights of old did braver deeds than I ask of you, to win favor at their ladies' hands——

GEN. But soft, fair Alice. How know you that I propose to do aught that would not bear the light of my countrymen's inspection? Burr has purchased the lands he now proposes to occupy. Surely, there no crime in that.

ALICE. You deceive yourself in seeking to deceive me. As I entered, you held a letter which you hastily concealed. The contents of that letter are known to me.

7

GEN. You are dreaming—the letter is in cypher (*searchingly*).

ALICE. Of which I have the key—shall I tell what is in the letter?

GEN. (*Confused.*) No, no.

ALICE. There is another person, a man, a remorseless enemy of Burr's, who also knows about the letter, knows who wrote it—to whom it is addressed and what is in it. It breathes treason in every line. If you retain that letter, and remain silent, your guilt is clear, you have but one course—denounce Burr, and save yourself——

GEN. And what may I hope for?

ALICE. For honor—instead of shame!

GEN. But you, sweet lady?

ALICE. As to myself, I promise nothing. It strikes me that if I were a man, I would be content for the moment in working the destruction of my rival.

GEN. You are right—I am yours——

ALICE. Then seal the compact. (*Holds out hand which General kisses.*)

ALICE. And now hasten to prepare for to-night's work.

GEN. You have set me a severe task, sweet lady ; but I do your bidding as a willing slave. (*Aside.*) The game is lost—she is right—there is but one course to pursue; I must save myself.

(*Exit, R.*)

ALICE. Now, my brave Colonel, you praised my beauty—if I do possess it, it has been a masked battery which now opens upon you.

(*Exit, L.*)

(SCENE CHANGES.)

SCENE III.

A ball-room in country house at Vicks-landing, near Wilkinson's head-quarters. Decorated in primitive style. Rustic guests discovered promenading.

(*Enter Blennerhassett, L. 2d.*)

BLENN. Although I cannot tell why, I feel a strange oppression on me this evening. (*Enter Mrs. Blennerhassett, R. 1st.*)

BLENN. Ah! my dear, I was wishing for you; as we near the consummation of our grand scheme I grow anxious and depressed.

MRS. B. (*R. C.*) What, at this glad time, when you should be so full of life. My dear husband, you must not give way to your despondency There is work to do. Why, shame on you, your wife is a better soldier than you are.

BLENN. I cannot repress the recurrence of that fearful dream. It still throws its pall about me. Reason as I may I cannot dispel the vague, uncertain apprehension that Burr will drag us down to ruin.

MRS. B. This is neither time nor place for such thoughts. They are but vagaries—Burr will be here presently, and we must greet him pleasantly as becomes the hour. (*Exit Mr. and Mrs. Blennerhassett.*)

Zekiel Green and Patience come on, (C. fr. R.) Zeke has an immense red favor in a bow-knot at his button-hole. Patience is grotesquely bedecked in the same color.

PATIENCE. What would they say, Zekiel, down into old Connecticut, if they could see us neow?

ZEKIEL. Aunt Patience, in addressing me hereafter, be kind enough to remember that I am a soldier and a captain.

PATIENCE. Go along, Zekiel, if you should be a brigadier, you would never be anything more to me than the boy I used to whollop years ago.

ZEKIEL. Aunt Patience, did you really used to whollop me?

PATIENCE. I did.

ZEKIEL. Then I have a mind to put you under arrest and get hunk on yeu for dewing it.

(*Enter Sambo and Paddy, C, f. R., wrangling. Sambo with huge red rosette. Paddy with green one.*)

SAM. Take it off, I tell you. What foh you wear dat green ribbon?

Pad. Phat color would you have me wear, you spalpeen ye !

Sam. You don't know noffin at all. Look at all de odder gemmin. Look at me. (*Strikes attitude.*)

Pad. Be me sowl, that's the very raison I wore the green. It's something British that's going on, so it is, and I wanted them to see that a son from the sod was always ready to stand by the country where the praties grow.

Sam. Now look a heah. Its nuffin ob de sort, yah ! yah ! You is a Irishman, you is. We's gwine to move down the ribber an capture Mexico, dats all ; we's gwine to took de entiah plantation, an' dey say we can plant some ob Mas' Aaron's gol' dus' and raise crops of big gol' money ! Min' what I say, if you don't took dat green jigger off and wear one like mine you won't get none of it. Ise tell you so.

Pat. Be jabers, is that the thruth, and will they devide up the money when it grows ?

Sam. Course dey will, course dey will. Everybody what wear a red ribbon will get heaps. Dis niggah no fool niggah. Yah, yah, Ise wear de ribbon. Look a heah. (*Takes red rosette from pocket.*) You'd better put dis on.

Pad. An' so 1 will. (*Takes ribbon and puts it in place of green one.*) But be me sowl, if I thought it was British, I'd never be afther doin' of a thing like this. (*They retire.*)

(*Music strikes up. Grand stir. Guests enter. Alice, Mr. and Mrs. Blenn. and rest. Burr follows dressed in full United States uniform of time. Blazing with gold. Barbaric device on breast, etc. They all bow to him. C.*)

Burr. (*C.*) This is an honor that I deserve as little as I expected it. I presume we are among friends. (*Looks all around and sees the red ribbons.*) I am assured of it, and I can continue what I was about to say. This is a moment when we should think of more serious subjects than the dance, but since it is as it is, and since this *fête* is given in my honor I can not honorably conceive any more appropriate manner of heralding the birth of

the new empire than by watching its glories pictured upon the
bubbles that float upon the surface of a wine glass, or harkening
to its prospective noise in the world as born to us on the music
of a band to night let our happiness be unalloyed.

ALICE. *Sweeping forward.*) Stay, Colonel Burr, the company
is not yet complete (*goes to back and beckons with handkerchief. L.
of arch door*)

BURR. (*Aside.*) She means mischief. She does not wear the
ribbon Well, let her do her worst.

(*Enter Nemo, conducting Margaret, C. fr. R.*)

ALICE (*L. C.*) Here is one who should share your tri
umph, Colonel Burr.

BURR. (*Aside to Alice.*) You are in bad company, fair Alice.
You must play a stronger card to thwart me now.

ALICE. Like a good player I reserve my trumps.

BURR. What! your one-armed knave? (*Glancing at Nemo*)

ALICE. No, the knave of trumps, you shall see.

MAR. (*Dazed.*) Where am I? They told me he was here
and wished for me—(*laughing wildly*)—ha, ha, ha! No, they have
mocked me, as they always do. He has gone to the wars and I
shall never see him again. (*Sings :*)

> O, if ever I were King of France,
> Or much better, Pope of Rome,
> I'd have no fighting men abroad
> Nor weeping maids at home.

(*Goes round to various persons and peers in their faces.*) But he
will come back, won't he? (*Peers into Burr's face—he stands un-
moved. She starts back, utters a scream.*) I said he would! I
said he would! (*Throws herself on his breast, sobbing. He pushes
her off.*)

BURR. Enough of this folly! Take this poor idiot away!

MAR. (*L. C.*) No, no, no! Don't send me away from you.

ALICE. (*L. C.*) Come to me, my poor child; you might as
well dash yourself against a stone image so far as his heart is concerned. That man is stone. (*Draws Margaret weeping away.*)
The honor of womanhood will not permit me to allow you to fawn
upon that man——

MAR. (*Piteously extending her arms.*) Aaron, Aaron, you will not let them separate me from you?

ALICE. I shall denounce you as a heartless villain.

BURR. (*Composedly, aside to her.*) Do so; you will find your effort futile.

ALICE. One and all listen to me. That poor shattered girl is that man's wife. (*Pointing to Burr.*) The man you are about to follow blindly. Do you not perceive he will but use you for his own selfish, cruel ends? You call yourselves men—will you stand by and witness his cruelty without condemning him? (*No one moves.*) Then you are as cold-hearted and as selfish as he. What magic spell binds you to that man?

BURR. You perceive, Miss Leighton, you but waste your energy. Aaron Burr soars above the storm a jealous woman raises——

ALICE. You flatter yourself with a false security——

(*Roll of drums heard without. General commotion.*)

BURR. What does that mean?

ALICE. It means retribution!

(*File of soldiers appear at back.*)

(*Enter Gen'l Wilkinson. C. fr. R.*)

BURR. (*Aside*) Without the ribbon! (*To Wilkinson.*) Speak sir. What does this mean. There is treason here!

GEN. (*R. C.*) There is. (*Aloud.*) Colonel Burr, I arrest you for high treason!

BURR. I am betrayed by a worthless dog—your charge is false sir! What proof have you?

GEN. This letter. (*Hands cypher letter.*)

BURR. I know knothing of it. It is in cypher.

ALICE. (*L.*) Perhaps Colonel Burr would like to have the key. (*Showing key to cypher.*)

BURR. Zounds, how did you get that! (*Recollecting himself.*) You trifle, you are deceived, this letter was not written by me.

ALICE. 'Tis false.

BURR. I dislike to contradict you, fair lady. but you know my hand ; pray glance at that.

ALICE. (*Takes letter hastily.*) He is right. It is not his writing. Have I been premature! Have I been played upon?

BURR. You have overreached yourself, my fair antagonist. Try again. Come, let the l all go on.

NEMO. Not so fast, not so fast! That is indeed a copy, but here is the original. (*Holds up paper. Alice snatches it from him.*)

ALICE. Perhaps you will deny this, too.

BURR. (*Seeking to take it. She holds it away.*) You are welcome to your victory, I can still afford to despise your duplicity.

GEN. (*Holding letter.*) Is that your writing ?

BURR. Do your duty ; I have nothing to say : my country will acquit me, and still revere the name of Aaron Burr.

NEMO. Not so ; you shall not live to baffle the meshes of the law. Look in my face ; do you read the secret of my hatred there ?

BURR. (*Agitated.*) Who are you ?

NEMO. Ask your culprit soul that question, and it will answer Hamilton and Margaret's avenger! (*Draws knife, and rushes upon Burr. Margaret, who has stealthily come down behind him, clings to his arm.*)

NEMO. (*Struggling.*) Let go, girl! You are mad, and know not what you do. (*In the struggle Margaret is stabbed, and falls mortally wounded. C.*)

NEMO. Poor, poor Margaret, speak to me but one word ere you die. Oh, God! I have killed you! But I shall follow thee even in death. (*Seizes knife, and stabs himself. Falls, L. C.*)

BURR. (*R. C. Looking at Margaret's form.*) I am sorry that when the eagle is snared the dove should likewise fall. (*Then glancing at Nemo's body.*) As for the dog, 'tis well that he should die ; he has had his day. (*To Alice.*) You may enjoy your triumph, most beautiful lady, and I have but to regret that my indifference to your charms has made you so potent an enemy. (*Alice starts and shudders with suppressed rage and shame. Burr turns to his followers.*) To you, good and brave men, in this hour of apparent gloom, when the star of empire seems paled by a rushlight, I give my thanks ; you have been loyal, and I am sure would have remained so at the extreme moment. The hands of the clock are stopped—but the hour will yet strike. (*To Wilkinson.*) If you could attain to the height of my scorn, I would express it. To be a traitor to your country is to be a traitor only when the alleged treason falls short of fruition. To be a traitor to a fellow man, and a friend, is certainly the most despicable of dishonorable acts. You are honored, sir, by having within the small compass of your being the province of arresting Colonel Burr. That duty will gild your name for all time. You are the mean associate of greatness fallen—though that greatness still remains. The sun shines upon the refuse of the barn yard—so will to-day's treachery illumine your name. I am ready, let us go.

CURTAIN.